Vroom!
Porsche

by August B. Arrigo IV

Ideas for Parents and Teachers

Bullfrog Books let children practice reading informational text at the earliest reading levels. Repetition, familiar words, and photo labels support early readers.

Before Reading
- Discuss the cover photo. What does it tell them?
- Look at the picture glossary together. Read and discuss the words.

During Reading
- "Walk" through the book with the reader. Discuss new or unfamiliar words. Sound them out together.
- Look at the photos together. Point out the photo labels.

After Reading
- Prompt the child to think more. Ask: Have you seen a Porsche? What color was it?

Bullfrog Books are published by Jump!
3500 American Blvd W, Suite 150
Bloomington, MN 55431
www.jumplibrary.com

Copyright © 2026 Jump! International copyright reserved in all countries. No part of this book may be reproduced in any form without written permission from the publisher.

Jump! is a division of FlutterBee Education Group.

Library of Congress Cataloging-in-Publication Data

Names: Arrigo, August B., IV, author.
Title: Porsche / by August B. Arrigo IV.
Description: Minneapolis, MN: Jump!, Inc., [2026]
Series: Vroom! | Includes index.
Audience: Ages 5–8
Identifiers: LCCN 2024058914 (print)
LCCN 2024058915 (ebook)
ISBN 9798896620266 (hardcover)
ISBN 9798896620273 (paperback)
ISBN 9798896620280 (ebook)
Subjects: LCSH: Porsche automobiles—Juvenile literature
Classification: LCC TL215.P75 A67 2026 (print)
LCC TL215.P75 (ebook
DDC 629.222/2—dc23/eng/20250202
LC record available at https://lccn.loc.gov/2024058914
LC ebook record available at https://lccn.loc.gov/2024058915

Editor: Jenna Gleisner
Designer: Anna Peterson

Photo Credits: Alexandre Prevot/Shutterstock, cover; August B. Arrigo IV, 1, 3, 14–15, 23tm, 23bl; Adam Berger, 4, 22, 23bm; Fabio Pagani/Shutterstock, 5; Marko583/Dreamstime, 6–7, 18–19; siekierski.photo/Shutterstock, 10–11, 23tr; Steve Neumayer, 12–13; Xinhua/Alamy, 16, 23tl; Gabo_Arts/Shutterstock, 17, 23br; Brandon Tang, 20–21, 24.

Printed in the United States of America at Corporate Graphics in North Mankato, Minnesota.

This book is dedicated to my little girls, Alivia and Alexandra, and instilling in them my love of Porsche.

Table of Contents

Cool Cars	4
Parts of a Porsche	22
Picture Glossary	23
Index	24
To Learn More	24

Porsche
(POR-shuh)

Cool Cars

Look! A Porsche.

Porsches are **sports cars**.

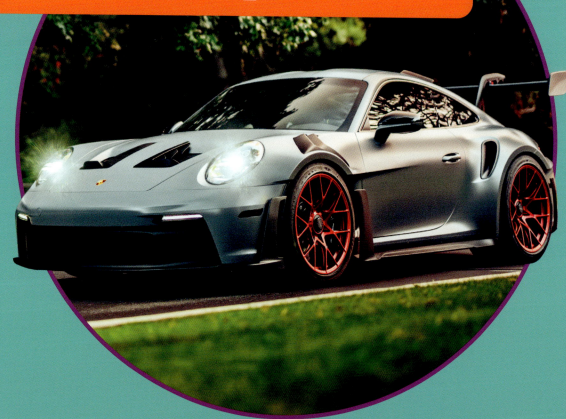

They are race cars, too!

The first Porsche was made in 1948.

It was called a 356.

These cars are made in Germany.

The **logo** is gold.

It has red and black stripes.

It has a horse.

The trunk can be in the front. It is called a frunk.

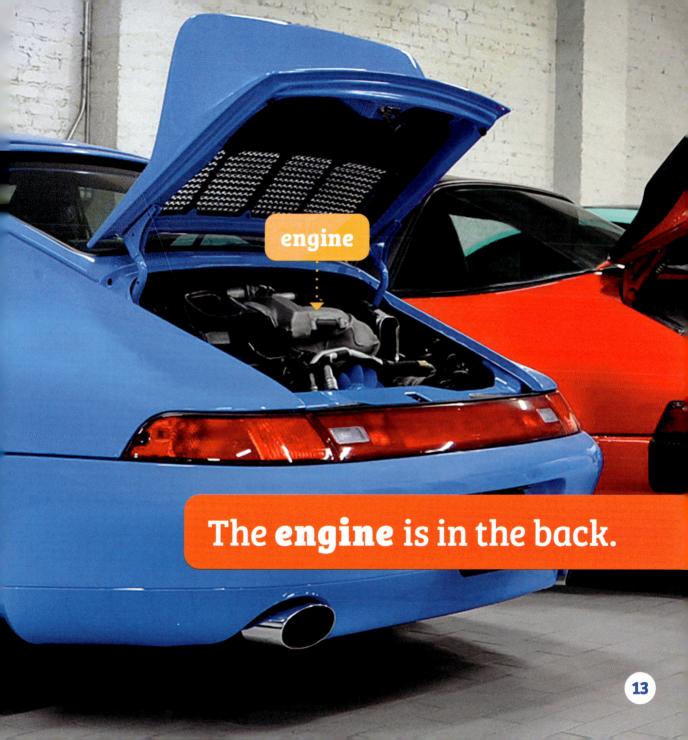

engine

The **engine** is in the back.

There are many **models**.

The 911 Carrera is sporty!

The Taycan is **electric**!

The Cayenne is an **SUV**.

This one is a Cabriolet.
The top can go down!
Cool!

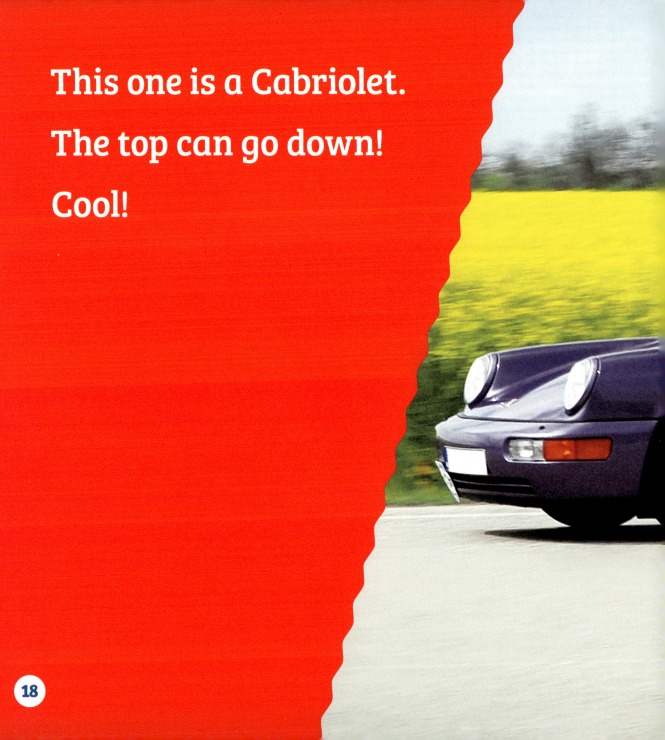

Porsches are for twisty roads!

Let's go fast!

Parts of a Porsche

A 2024 Porsche 911 GT3 RS model can go almost 200 miles (322 kilometers) per hour! Take a look at the parts of a Porsche!

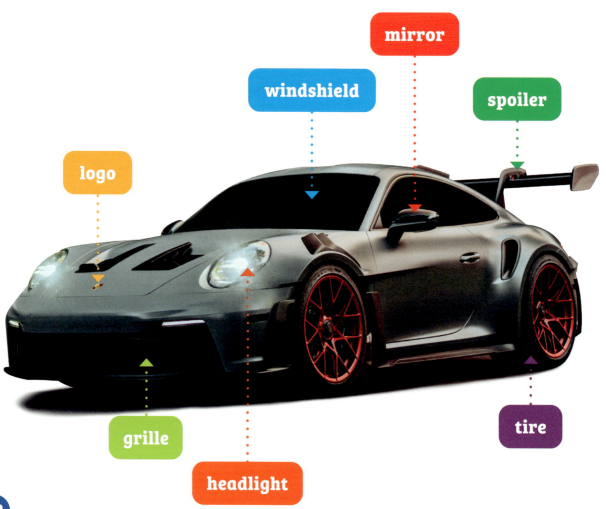

Picture Glossary

electric
Using electricity for power.

engine
A machine that makes something move by using gasoline or another energy source.

logo
A symbol that stands for a company.

models
Particular types or designs.

sports cars
Cars that are made to go fast and handle turns well.

SUV
Short for Sport Utility Vehicle. A car that can drive where there are no roads.

Index

Cabriolet 18
Cayenne 17
engine 13
frunk 12
Germany 9
logo 10
models 14
911 Carrera 14
race cars 5
sports cars 4
Taycan 16
356 6

To Learn More

Finding more information is as easy as 1, 2, 3.

❶ Go to www.factsurfer.com

❷ Enter **"Porsche"** into the search box.

❸ Choose your book to see a list of websites.